THOMAS PAINE'S
LEWES

Judy Moore

S.B. Publications

Thomas Paine

First published in 2000 by S. B. Publications
c/o 19 Grove Road, Seaford, Sussex BN25 1TP
telephone 01323 893498: fax 01323 893860
Email sales@sbpublications.swinternet.co.uk

© JEM
Design/typesetting, JEM Editorial – JEMedit@AOL.com.uk

ISBN 1 85770 207 7

Printed by Tansleys the Printers
19 Broad Street
Seaford
East Sussex BN25 1LS
01323 891019

Cover picture of Lewes Bowling Green by Toby Canham

THE APOSTLE

OF FREEDOM

Thomas Paine, the Apostle of Freedom, was a politician, writer and prophet, scorned during most of his lifetime for ideas since adopted without acknowledgement. He is today recognised as the prime mover of two of the world's greatest revolutions. England, America and France each claimed him as a citizen and each ultimately rejected him. George Washington said that Paine was 'one of the greatest of all the forces that brought about, sustained and carried to a successful conclusion, the American War of Independence'. Thomas Edison called him 'the real founder of the American Republic', and a contemporary observer wrote: 'The great American cause owed as much to the pen of Paine as to the sword of Washington'.

The first person to use the phrase 'the United States of America' was Thomas Paine, in the third of his Crisis pamphlets

The life of Paine has been dissected, discussed and analysed in books (and, now, on websites) by the score, most of which have him materialising centre-stage in the New World, fully-formed, at one of the great moments of history.

Yet Paine had already lived more than half his life before he set foot in America – to which he fled penniless and ruined. His life thus far had been unpromising, with barely a hint of the powerful expression of radical ideas that were to inflame two continents. By some quirk of fate this argumentative, twice-dismissed excise officer and failed shop-keeper, whose greatest ambition at the time was to find work as a schoolmaster, stepped ashore at Philadelphia in 1774, and into the history books. By a second quirk of fate he died in poverty and obscurity, ignored by the American people whose freedom he had won.

What sort of man was he? He left little information about himself – volumes of autobiographical material went missing after his death – and he was reticent in conversation with companions. According to his friend Joel Barlow:

> 'He was one of the most instructive men I ever have known. He had a surprising memory and brilliant fancy; his mind was a storyhouse of facts and useful observations; he was full of lively anecdote, and ingenious, original, pertinent remarks upon almost every subject.'

The world is my country, to do good my religion.
Thomas Paine

Lord Edward Fitzgerald, who served as Paine's interpreter in France when he pleaded for the life of Louis XVI, described Paine in a letter to his mother:

> 'The more I see of his interior, the more I like and respect him. I cannot express how kind he is to me; there is a simplicity of manner, a goodness of heart, and a strength of mind in him, that I never knew a man before possess.'

His friend and biographer Clio Rickman said Paine was an 'elegant and a courageous sportsman on ice and in the water' and a man of 'easy and gracious manners'. Broad shouldered and of athletic build, he was an expert horseman, loved music, sang well and enjoyed long country walks.

Thomas Paine: a copy of the lost Romney portrait of 1792
SUSSEX ARCHAEOLOGICAL SOCIETY COLLECTIONS

4

LEWES IN THOMAS PAINE'S DAY

Paine's last home in England was in Lewes, where he lived with his wife Elizabeth, worked as an excise officer and ran a shop selling tobacco and groceries.

This county seat of Sussex was, then, the place where the local landed gentry owned magnificent town houses – to which they moved each winter for a season of glittering assemblies, concerts and plays.

Lewes has been a busy meeting and trading place since Saxon times; it became a focus for the professions from mediaeval days and evolved into an important administrative and legal centre. Lawyers, physicians and surgeons settled in Lewes to attend to the needs of the gentry, banks opened and schools for the sons of the wealthy multiplied. It was, too, an agricultural centre, with cattle and corn markets, a sheep fair and an annual fatstock show. Corn and wool merchants, saddlers, blacksmiths and gunsmiths set up in the town to cater for farmers' needs.

Traders used the river – once navigable by sea-going vessel as far north as Lewes – to export wool, grain and Wealden iron to Europe and to import spices, wines, textiles and tobacco, Baltic timber and coal from Tyneside, lace from Bruges, rhubarb from Russia, citrus fruits from the Mediterranean and cheese from Holland.

The town was well provided with malthouses and breweries and had many, many inns and taverns. And there were makers

Toleration is not the opposite of Intolerance, but it is the counterfeit of it. The one assumes to itself the right of with-holding Liberty of Conscience, and the other of granting it.
Thomas Paine

Defoe's 'open champaign country on the edge of the South Downs'. A view of Lewes from the west. The cleft in the Downs is the Coombe, known locally, for obvious reasons, as Fat Belly Woman.

and traders of clocks and screws, velvets and linens, periwigs and marble grave stones – indeed anything the Lewes residents could possibly want.

Georgian England was a time of prosperity and, in line with the fashion of the day, owners of houses lining Lewes High Street gentrified them with new facades in the classical style. Behind many of these eighteenth century fronts are the timbered houses of Tudor times. An easily-seen example is Barbican House, Sussex Archaeological Society's museum beside the castle.

The entertainment of the time included cock-fighting in tavern yards; bull and bear baiting; bare-fisted prize-fighting below the Coombe. Cricket was played on Cliffe Hill and at Houndean Bottom, a three-day race meeting was a social highlight each summer and there was excellent fishing for salmon, trout and eels in the Ouse. Gentlemen kept packs of hounds for hunting, and plentiful wildfowl on the watermeadows provided sport for the guns.

The activity that most engaged Paine's leisure time was bowling at the old Castle Yard and here, as in most other sports at that time, heavy wagers were placed.

Daniel Defoe visited Lewes in 1722 and wrote:

'Lewes is a fine pleasant town, well built, agreeably situated in the middle of an open champaign country, and on the edge of the South Downs, the pleasantest, and most delightful of their kind in the nation; it lies on the bank of a little wholesome fresh river, within twelve miles of the sea, but that which adds to the character of this town, is, that both the town and the country adjacent, is full of gentlemen of good families and fortunes.'

'You can see Lewes lying like a box of toys under a great amphitheatre of chalk hills . . . on the whole it is set down better than any town I have seen in England,' William Morris wrote.

And Paine's disciple, William Cobbett, in *Rural Rides*, described Lewes as a town of clean windows and pretty girls.

Morris's 'box of toys' is still apparent from the hills around, or the top of the castle keep and in spite of some unsympathetic twentieth century developments Thomas Paine's Lewes is still there to be discovered.

Houses at Westgate

7

FROM CORSETS

TO CUSTOMS

For the domestic happiness of Britain and the peace of the world, I wish she had not a foot of land but what is circumscribed within her own island. Extend of dominion has been her ruin, and instead of civilizing others has brutalized herself.

Thomas Paine

Thomas Paine was born on January 29, 1737, at Thetford, Norfolk. His artisan father, Joseph Pain (Thomas added the 'e' when he left England), was a stay-maker – he made whalebone or steel stiffeners for women's corsets. He also had a small farm. Thomas's mother, Frances, a lawyer's daughter, was eleven years older than Joseph and was said to be a difficult, sour woman. She was nearly forty when Thomas was born. The boy, their only child after a daughter, Elizabeth, died as a baby, left the local grammar school at thirteen to learn the intricacies of stay-making with his father.

When he was sixteen he ran away from the dull life and demeaning job in Thetford, and at Harwich joined the privateer *Terrible*, under Captain William Death. Many years later Paine wrote:

'Raw and adventurous, and heated with the false heroism of a (school) master who had served in a man-o-war, I became the carver of my own fortune, and entered on board the Terrible privateer, Capt. Death. From this adventure I was happily prevented by the affectionate and moral remonstrance of a good father, who, from his own habits of life, being of the Quaker profession, must begin to look upon me as lost.'

Those were dangerous times, when England and France were both contending for empire in India and America, and bloody battle raged on the high seas. The privateers were armed vessels, privately owned, authorised by government to raid the merchant ships of hostile nations and seize cargos for their own profit. Letters of marque and reprisal distinguished these seamen from ordinary pirates and saved them from the hangman's noose if captured. On the sailing from which young Paine had been rescued by his father, the *Terrible* lost 172 of her 200 crew in a battle with the French privateer *Vengeance.*

Three years later he again made a bid for freedom, this time succeeding in escaping to sea as a cabin boy on the privateer *King of Prussia*, under Captain Mendez. The ship was a large man-o'-war with two gun decks, and she carried a crew of some 250 men.

After an eighteen-month voyage – of which he never spoke – Paine left the sea and went back to his old trade, this time working as a journeyman stay-maker for John Morris in London. In 1758 he moved to a position in Dover and the following year he went to Sandwich in Kent, where he opened his own shop with £10 given him by his generous Dover employer, a Mr Grace. Here he married Mary Lambert, a maidservant, on September 27, 1759.

His business was not a success and, burdened by debts, he and Mary ran away with a few of their belongings one dark night as creditors were hammering on the door. They settled nearby in Margate where, less than a year later, Mary died, possibly in childbirth.

Bereft, the young widower resolved finally to abandon a calling he had always disliked, and make a new life for himself in a new place.

Paine had been intrigued by Mary's stories of her father's adventurous life as an excise officer. He took his late father-in-law's books, went home to Thetford and studied for the Board of Excise examination.

The excise was a customs duty (a 'hateful tax' according to Dr Johnson) on alcohol, tobacco, tea, salt, soap and some grocery items. Excise men spent long hours on the road, and were

I am proud to say that with a perseverance undismayed by difficulties, a disinterestedness that compelled respect, I have not only contributed to raise a new empire in the world, founded on a new system of government, but I have arrived at an eminence in political literature, the most difficult of all lines to succeed and excel in, which aristocracy, with all its aids, has not been able to reach or to rival.

Thomas Paine

often attacked by smugglers and thieves. They were required to file written reports to the Board of Excise in London, and to collect the tax. Paine passed the examinations and was appointed a junior officer, initially to gauge brewers' casks at Grantham in Linconshire.

Later he moved to Alford, in the same county, where often he risked his life in confrontations with smugglers. The illegal import of otherwise ruinously-taxed 'luxury' items was regarded with some favour by eager-to-buy citizens, who allied themselves with the smugglers in considering excise men to be 'odious'.

The excise officer of the day was distinguished by the ink bottle hanging from his buttonhole, and his measuring stick, which was covered with figures.

Just a year after he arrived at Alford Paine was dismissed for 'stamping' – accepting a tradesman's word for the amount of taxable goods he had in stock without himself checking.

Accused of having 'stampt his whole ride', he confessed his guilt and was discharged in August 1765.

When opinions are free, either in matters of government or of religion, truth will finally and powerfully prevail.

Thomas Paine

An eighteenth century riding officer, supported by Dragoons, on the trail of Sussex smugglers

THE LEWES
RIDING OFFICER

For a year or so Paine barely made a living. He worked first as a stay-maker at Diss in Norfolk, then taught English at two schools in London. Unable to find security, he petitioned his former employers at the Board of Excise for reinstatement, humiliating himself with his humble begging, and concluding his letter: 'I will endeavour that my future conduct shall as much engage your honours' approbation as my former has merited your displeasure'.

His humility won the day and in February 1768, aged thirty-one, Paine was appointed to the Lewes 4 Outride, where he was to be one of six riding officers. His annual salary was £50, and from this he had to maintain a horse, pay for his lodgings, feed and clothe himself. It was, Paine later wrote, barely enough to keep a man alive.

Paine may have been recommended to seek lodgings with tobacconist Samuel Ollive and his wife Esther at Bull House, in the High Street, by the master of the White Hart Inn, Thomas Scrace. As well as being an inn-keeper, Scrace was also the official keeper of the local excise office, from which nine excisemen worked. It has been suggested that, at the time, Paine had strong Methodist leanings (although his father was a Quaker, and his mother Church of England), and had even, unsuccessfully, sought ordination as a Methodist minister. Thus a room in the nonconformist Ollive household would best suit him.

Public money ought to be touched with the utmost scrupulousness of honour. It is not the produce of riches only, but of the hard savings of labour and poverty. It is drawn even from the bitterness of want and misery. Not a beggar passes, or perishes in the streets, whose mite is not in that mass.
Thomas Paine

Church of St Michael-in-Lewes

At Bull House Paine occupied a room on the upper floor. He slipped easily into Lewes society, despite his despised profession. This may have been achieved through his respected landlord, Ollive, twice an elected High Constable of the Borough. Ollive was Thomas Paine's sponsor with the congregation of Westgate Chapel, a nonconformist place of worship attached to the rear of Bull House, and his association with the popular shopkeeper paved the way for Paine's early election to a 'jury' of twelve prominent citizens who managed town affairs.

Some of the friends he made in Lewes stayed close to him throughout his life. One was Henry Verrall, who ran the Whig coffee house at Newcastle House from 1742 to 1779, and who also managed the Assembly Room from 1764. Another Lewes friend was Thomas 'Clio' Rickman, but, as he was only six years old when Paine arrived in the town and thirteen when he left, it is unlikely the two knew each other then, as some biographers have claimed. Rickman was the classically educated son of John Rickman, the Quaker brewer at Bear Yard in the Cliffe. Paine and Rickman met in London in 1792. Rickman had set up business in the capital in 1785, as a printer and bookseller, and established his political and literary credentials by naming his sons Paine, Washington, Franklin, Rousseau, Petrarch and Volney. Paine lodged in Rickman's London house to write *Rights of Man*.

In his biography of his friend, Rickman wrote:

'In this place (Lewes) he lived several years in habits of intimacy with a very respectable, sensible, and convivial set of acquaintance, who were entertained with his witty sallies and informed by his more serious conversation. In politics he was at this time a Whig, and notorious for that quality which has been defined perseverance in a good cause and obstinacy in a bad one. He was tenacious of his opinions, which were bold, acute and independent, and which he maintained with ardour, elegance and argument.'

The fact that Paine preserved his popularity in Lewes, albeit an exciseman, and was accepted so easily into society, must have meant that he carried out his duties with a good deal of tact. Tea-drinking in particular had become a national habit and, a few years later, Prime Minister William Pitt calculated that 'thirteen million pounds of tea were consumed in the kingdom, of which only five and a half millions had paid duty'.

Benjamin Franklin said: 'Where liberty is, there is my country'. Thomas Paine said: 'Where liberty is not, there is my country'.

'Perhaps,' Audrey Williamson, his 1972 biographer wrote, 'Paine did turn a blind eye to the activities of some of the Lewes inhabitants and accepted any cups of tea offered him philosophically, without comment.'

Bull House and the entrance to Westgate Chapel

13

That he undertook his duties with some compassion seems evident from a letter he sent to Lewes from London, after his return from America. It was about a meeting to be held in the town to protest against a royal proclamation suppressing seditious writings.

'It is now upwards of eighteen years since I was a resident inhabitant of the town of Lewes. My situation among you as an officer of the revenue, for more than six years, enabled me to see into the numerous and various distresses which the weight of taxes even at that time of day occasioned; and feeling, as I then did, and as it is natural for me to do, for the hard condition of others, it is with pleasure I can declare, and every person then under my survey, and now living, can witness the exceeding candour, and even tenderness, with which that part of the duty that fell to my share was executed . . . Many of you will recollect, that whilst I resided among you, there was not a man more firm and open in supporting the principles of liberty than myself, and I still pursue, and ever will, the same path.'

Thomas Paine as menu holder at the White Hart Hotel

Said Rickman: 'At this period, at Lewes, the White Hart evening club was the resort of a social and intelligent circle who, out of fun, seeing that disputes often ran very warm and high, frequently had what they called the "Headstrong Book". This was no other than an old Greek Homer which was sent the morning after a debate vehemently maintained, to the most obstinate haranguer in the club; . . . Mr. Pain . . . best deserved and most frequently obtained it.'

A prophetic, anonymous piece of verse was devised to accompany the book as it was, morning after morning, conveyed along the High Street from the White Hart to Bull House.

> '*Immortal Paine, while mighty reasoners jar*
> *We crown thee General of the Headstrong War;*
> *Thy logic vanquished error, and thy mind*

No bounds but those of right and truth confined.
Thy soul of fire must sure ascend the sky,
Immortal Paine, thy fame can never die;
For men like thee their names must ever save
From the black edits of the tyrant grave.

His issues were often unpopular – justice for women, the abolition of slavery, international arbitration. Sometimes his only supporters were Quakers. Perhaps the origins of the pamphlets and books which were, in later life, to flow from his trenchant pen, began here amid the discussions of the Headstrong Club in the old oak-panelled upper room at the White Hart. Usually the talk was convivial, but there were times when Paine voiced his disenchantment with the established order of things. He ranted particularly against the 'rotten boroughs', and joined the growing voice demanding greater freedom and a widening of the franchise.

Wine and brandy – stamped, perhaps, by Paine the excise officer – flowed during these discussions, and quantities of oysters were consumed as conversation ranged over matters of the moment.

Clio Rickman

While in Lewes Paine wrote a campaign song for a politician called Rumbold, New Shoreham's Whig candidate to Parliament, for which he was paid three guineas; and an elegy on the death of General James Wolfe, killed in the Battle of Quebec. This first appeared in print in 1775 in the *Pennsylvania Magazine*, which Paine edited, but it was written in Lewes.

In different vein, he wrote a humorous poem, *Farmer Short's*

Remains of the West Gate of Lewes; on the left, Bull House and Westgate Chapel

15

Dog Porter: A Tale, which told of a farmer who voted in an election for candidates not favoured by the local justices of the peace. Because they could not charge Farmer Short with any crime they charged his dog:

> *That he, this dog, did then and there*
> *Pursue, and take, and kill a hare;*
> *Which treason was, or some such thing,*
> *Against our Sovereign Lord the King.*

The poem ends, after much beating about the bush, and several verses later, with the hanging of the poor dog.

> *This logic, rhetoric, and wit,*
> *So nicely did the matter hit,*
> *That Porter, though unheard, was cast,*
> *And in a halter breathed his last.*
> *And the justices? Why, they*
> *Adjourned to dine*
> *And whet their logic up with wine.*

The other activity that occupied Paine's time was membership of the Lewes Bowling Green Club, which was founded in 1753. Lewes people enjoy a harmless conceit that it was here he was inspired to plan revolution, and pen *Rights of Man,* the 'seditious' book he published in 1787. Sadly for the tourist industry, the dates conflict, but according to Paine's 1819 biographer, William Sherwin:

> 'He happened one day to be playing at Bowls with some friends at Lewes; after they had finished playing, they went to a neighbouring house to drink some punch by way of refreshment. Mr. Verral, one of the bowlers, observed, in allusion to the wars of Frederick "that the King of Prussia was the best fellow in the world for a king, he had so much of the devil in him". This observation, trifling as it might appear, produced a very deep impression on the mind of Paine and gave rise to the reflection, that if it were necessary for a king to have so much of the devil in him kings might very well be dispensed with. This, quite unintentionally, gave him the idea of writing "The Rights of Man".'

The bowling green on the old tilting yard

Samuel Ollive died in 1769, leaving a widow, two young sons and a daughter, Elizabeth. There was a meeting of Ollive's creditors at the White Hart, and the *Lewes Journal* carried a notice advertising that all his possessions, professional, domestic and personal, were about to come under the hammer. Every stick of furniture and every thread of linen was sold to satisfy the creditors. Within days the *Journal* carried another notice, this one inserted by Paine and Ollive's schoolteacher daughter, Elizabeth. It would appear that Paine had decided to step in and help the widow and her children by taking on the shop in partnership with the mother and daughter. The notice said:

> 'Thomas Pain and Eliz. Ollive, Daughter of the late Mr. Sam. Ollive, near the West-Gate, Lewes, continue selling in the same shop, all sorts of TOBACCO, SNUFF, CHEESE, BUTTER and Home-made BACON, with every Article of GROCERY, (TEA excepted) Wholesale and Retail, at the lowest Prices.

'An entire new Stock will be laid in as soon as the present Stock, now advertised for public Sale, can be disposed of.'

Paine moved out of Bull House for propriety's sake, and helped run the shop when he could, by keeping the accounts and by buying, milling and shredding tobacco. He expanded the stock to include groceries and distilled spirits. The exception of tea among the stock was possibly to avoid objections from his employers at the excise office, tea being a staple commodity of smugglers.

Because their pay was so poor, it was common for revenue officers to take another occupation – or turn to corruption. Indeed, it was believed by their superiors that many excisemen profited from seized contraband – a reason for not increasing their pay – and because of their otherwise hand-to-mouth existence, that is what many tax men were forced to do. The scale of smuggling in Sussex was that of a large, well-organised industry

During Paine's six years in Lewes – a long period for the wanderer – he took his first steps in politics. Within just a few months he was a member of the Society of Twelve, which elected two new Constables and two new Headboroughs each year to administer the affairs of the town, and he also took part in meetings of St Michael's Vestry, a group convened to provide funds for the upkeep of the church and the assistance of widows, orphans and others in need. His introduction to Lewes's leading players came through Ollive, himself one of the two Constables, with Henry Verrall, when Paine arrived in the town.

On March 26, 1771 Paine married Elizabeth at St Michael-in-Lewes, and moved back into Bull House where he became a full partner, as Elizabeth's husband, in the running of the tobacco and snuff business. Two years earlier, Elizabeth, aged nineteen, had opened a boarding school for young ladies 'at Mr. Feron's, two Doors above Verral's Coffee-House, in Lewes: where all those who shall please to favour her with their Children, may depend upon the greatest Care taken of them'.

There were a number of clay pipe makers in Lewes between the seventeenth and nineteenth centuries. Customers of the tobacco shop at Bull House were most likely to have used pipes made by the Harman family who had their premises nearby in the High Street.

18

She had trained under a Mrs Ridge, who had lately given up her own school in Lewes.

It appears to have been a marriage of convenience. One possible reason was to still tongues when Paine moved back into the house with the two women. The Ollive women gained the protection of a man in the house and Paine, the wanderer, acquired a home. The marriage was never consummated; neither Paine, nor Elizabeth ever talked about the circumstances, although Paine admitted later that he 'married for prudential reasons and abstained for prudential reason'. He told Rickman: 'I had cause for it, but I will name it to no one'. Apparently, years later, Rickman spoke on the subject with a Lewes doctor who had treated Paine, and was told that non-consummation was not due to any physical defect on Paine's part.

Lewes Castle

Whether Paine was celibate or not from the age of thirty-four, he believed in the state of matrimony; in a letter written in 1789 to the newly-married Kitty Nicholson, the daughter of a friend, he wrote:

'Though I appear a sort of wanderer, the married state has not a sincerer friend than I am. It is the harbour of human life, and is, with respect to the things of this world, what the next world is to this. It is home; and that one word conveys more than any other word can express. For a few years we may glide along the tide of youthful single life, and be wonderfully delighted; but it is a tide that flows but once, and what is still worse, it ebbs faster than it flows, and leaves many a hapless voyager around.

'I am one, you see, that have experienced the fate I am describing. I have lost my tide; it passed by while every thought of my heart was on the wing for the salvation of my dear America, and I have now as contentedly as I can, made myself a little bower of willows on the shore that has the solitary resemblance of a home.'

*Every
community has
a right to
demand of all
its agents an
account of
their
conduct.*

Thomas Paine

The Barbican c1760 PRINT FROM THE HISTORY AND ANTIQUITIES OF LEWES, HORSFIELD

In 1772 Paine became involved in the excise officers' campaign for a salary increase. He took up the cause and agreed to be the officers' representative in a petition to Parliament. His pamphlet, *Case of the Officers of Excise*, argued for justice and the eradication of abuses in a restrained, respectful and logical manner.

Using money raised to promote the campaign, Paine moved to London, without the permission of the Board of Excise, to promote the cause – even though it soon became obvious that nothing would come of it.

In the capital he was introduced to the American printer, publisher, inventor and scientist, Benjamin Franklin, then Pennsylvania's agent in London. Franklin, and Paine's friend and patron, George Lewis Scott, a commissioner of the Board of Excise, sparked his interest in science and he spent the winter of 1772-1773 attending scientific lectures, conversing with new political friends, learning the mysteries of astronomy. Later, he wrote:

> 'After I had . . . conceived an idea of the infinity of space, and of the eternal divisibility of matter, and obtained, at least, a general knowledge of what was called natural philosphy, I began to compare, or . . . to confront, the internal evidence these things afford with the Christian system of faith.'

The campaign for his fellow officers failed and Paine returned to Lewes to find his shop on the brink of insolvency, and the excise board anxious to examine his books – in which there were only empty pages. The shop, something of a failure when he *was* in Lewes, simply folded during his long sojourn in London. 'Trade I do not understand,' he admitted.

In April of 1774 Paine was again dismissed from the service, officially for 'having quitted his business without obtaining the Board's leave for so doing, and having gone off on account of the debts which he hath constructed'. Unofficially, the *Case of the Officers of Excise* may also have had something to do with his dismissal, not to mention the incompatibility of trading in excisable commodities, by which Paine had compromised his position. William Cobbett declared that this dismissal was the real cause of the American Revolution.

Benjamin Franklin

Paine and his wife had to sell all they owned to pay their creditors – although this did not include Bull House, which remained the property of Samuel Ollive's widow until she died, after which its value was divided between her three children. A poster advised that 'all the household furniture, stock in trade and other effects of Thomas Pain, grocer and tobacconist' were to be auctioned. 'Also a horse, a tobacco and snuff mill, with all the utensils for cutting tobacco and grinding off snuff; and two unopened crates of cream-coloured stone ware.'

This is the most widely accepted account of how Paine came to leave Lewes, but there is another version, from Paine scholar G Hindmarch. This says that early in 1774 Paine had been recommended for promotion, probably by George Lewis Scott, and that he was preparing to move away from Lewes. The notice in the *Lewes Journal* advertising the sale of all his possessions appeared on April 11. Hindmarch guesses at perhaps a week between insertion and publication; thus notification of an auction of Paine's property, preparatory to his moving out of town to a new position, would have been inserted in the *Journal* on April 3 or 4. Paine was dismissed on April 8.

Hindmarch claims that there is strong circumstantial evidence of Paine's ruin being contrived. The Excise Collector for Sussex, Paine's superior, was away, and his place had been taken temporarily by Edward Clifford, sent from London on April 6. Within two days of his arrival in Lewes he had laid a complaint about Paine's absence without leave, the complaint was taken to London and on April 8, Paine was discharged.

At that time Paine and Elizabeth, who had been married for three years, separated legally, 'she engaging to pay her husband thirty-five pounds (presumably part of whatever was left after debts had been settled), and he promising to claim no part of whatever goods she might gain in the future (ie a share of Bull House, on the death of her mother)'. They were never divorced, and thereafter 'spoke only kindly of each other'. Many years later, when Paine heard that Elizabeth needed money, he 'sent her several times pecuniary aid, without her knowing even whence it came,' according to Clio Rickman. Throughout her life, Elizabeth maintained that Paine was 'ever kind and considerate'.

It is not known how long Elizabeth continued with her school. In 1793 she was recorded as a mantua-maker, living near London, and eventually she went to live with her brother Thomas, a watchmaker, in Cranbrook, Kent. She died in 1808, eight months before Paine's own death.

The right to property being inviolable and sacred, no one ought to be deprived of it, except in cases of evident public necessity, legally ascertained, and on conditions of a previous just indemnity.
Thomas Paine

Penniless, with no home, deprived of his livelihood, separated from Elizabeth and with his life in ruins at thirty-seven, Paine returned to London. He told Franklin that he wished to start a new life in America, where he dreamed of setting up an academy for young ladies. A failed stay-maker, disastrous shopkeeper and twice-dismissed excise officer, Paine, nearing forty, appeared to have little to offer. Certainly there was scant evidence that he was to become a world-shaking thinker and writer. Yet Franklin must have perceived some spark, for he provided a letter of introduction to his son-in-law, Richard Bache, a merchant in Philadelphia, recommending Paine as 'an ingenious worthy young man'. The letter added:

'He goes to Pennsylvania with a view of settling there. I request you to give him your best advice and countenance, as he is quite a stranger there. If you can put him in a way of obtaining employment as a clerk, or assistant tutor in a school, or assistant surveyor, of all of which I think him very capable, so that he may procure a subsistence at least, till he can make an acquaintance and obtain a knowledge of the country, you will do well, and much oblige your affectionate father.'

It is time that nations should be rational, and not governed, like animals, for the pleasure of their riders.
Thomas Paine

A MYSTERIOUS
FORESTER

All religions are in their nature kind and benign and united with principles of morality.

Thomas Paine

Within weeks of arriving in America Thomas Paine was working as a journalist having never, as he claimed, 'published a syllable in England in my life' – with the exception, of course, of *Case of the Officers of Excise* and the doggerel about the farmer's dog.

Yet G Hindmarch, in his essay *Thomas Paine: The Methodist Influence* (from a 1979 edition of the Thomas Paine Society's *Bulletin)*, maintains that Paine published some forty articles in the form of letters in the *Sussex Weekly Advertiser* and the *Lewes Journal*, under the pen name of A Forester. The 'novel, provocative views and the mastery of the written word' proclaimed these pieces as being from Paine's pen, Hindmarch says. The dates, too, coincide with Paine's residence in Lewes, and the name, 'A Forester', is all but the same as 'The Forester', a nom-de-plume that Paine later used in America.

Examples given by Hindmarch include:

'The universal veneration men have for the mineral call'd Gold is highly absurd and preposterous.'

'Life is life, though it be in miniature, and it's nothing but ignorance and prejudice that makes you think a creature beneath your notice, only because it's less than yourself.'

'When we see a child in raptures over a piece of gilt gingerbread, we see a PICTURE OF THE TIMES.'

But George Spate, writing in the *Bulletin* in 1982, says that A Forester was 'too classical' for Paine. The articles include the words of Ovid, Virgil and Horace in the original Latin. Thomas Paine's writings 'are devoid of such literary embellishment, and he rarely quoted authors,' Spate says.

Long after Paine had left Lewes, a second group of A Forester articles appeared in the *Sussex Weekly Advertiser* and the *Lewes Journal*, between 1787 and 1789.

On February 1, 1790, the *Advertiser* carried an obituary for the Reverend Richard Michell, 'of East-Dean, author of the many letters . . . under the signature of A Forester'.

It is, of course, possible that there were two A Foresters . .

I believe that religious duties consist in doing justice, loving mercy, and endeavouring to make our fellow creatures happy.
Thomas Paine

WITH PEN
AND MUSKET

With how much more glory, and advantage to itself, does a nation act, when it exerts its power to rescue the world from bondage, and to create itself friends, than when it employs those powers to increase ruin, desolation and misery?
Thomas Paine

Paine used the £35 given him by Elizabeth to travel first class on the *London Packet*, which sailed to America in October 1774. He arrived in the New World at a time of seething unrest. The colonists were in ferment over unfair taxes and George III had sent troops under the command of General Gage – from Firle, near Lewes – to quell the unruly Americans.

In Philadelphia Paine helped Robert Aitkin to set up the *Pennsylvania Magazine*. He became its editor and began a series of articles on justice, and freedom from royal, ecclesiastical and hereditary privilege. His forty-seven page pamphlet *Common Sense*, published in Philadelphia on February 9, 1776, was the first open declaration calling for independence from England. Everybody who could read, read it, and the unknown author was hailed as 'an angel from heaven'.

'On the 1st of January a word was spoken by a poor vagrant stay-maker: by the 4th of July it had been repeated from Vermont even to Georgia; on that day the Independence of thirteen states was proclaimed; a home, and rallying place, was established for Freedom; and from that day to this, far-throned monarchy has not ceased to quail, in sad presentiment of its assured doom.'
So wrote 'The Editor of The National' in his 1842 *Life of Paine*.

The generals and the politicians may already have thought the unthinkable, but it was Paine, newly arrived from England, who appealed, publicly, to the ordinary people of America to free themselves from the yoke of British imperialism. There was only one course for the colonists to take, he argued, and that was to effect complete separation from England.

Almost overnight he swung moderate opinion. George Washington maintained that *Common Sense* was the reason for his own conversion to the cause of independence, and the prime moving cause in the war that secured that independence.

The pamphlet ran to more than 120,000 copies within three months. It stirred up the revolution, and was followed by a series of publications, all entitled *Crisis,* which kept up morale among civilians and the troops mustered under Washington to fight General Gage's soldiers.

Paine joined up, writing the first *Crisis* on the march. Washington, it is said, called his exhausted, shattered soldiers together just before the desperate bid for victory at Trenton, and read the pamphlet to them.

It famously begins:

> 'These are times that try men's souls. The summer soldier and the sunshine patriot will, in this crisis, shrink from the service of their country; but he that stands *now*, deserves the love and thanks of man and woman. Tyranny, like Hell, is not easily conquered; yet we have this consolation with us, that the harder the conflict, the more glorious the triumph. What we obtain too cheap, we esteem too lightly: it is dearness only that gives everything its value. Heaven knows how to put a proper price upon its goods: and it would be strange indeed if so celestial an article as Freedom should not be highly rated.'

Trenton was won.

I am thus far a Quaker, that I would gladly agree with all the world to lay aside the use of arms, and settle matters by negotiations; but unless the whole world will, the matter ends, and I take up my musket and thank heaven he has put it in my power.

Thomas Paine

SATAN'S EMISSARY

One of the strongest natural proofs of the folly of hereditary right in kings, is, that nature disapproves it, otherwise she would not so frequently turn it into ridicule by giving mankind an ass for a lion.

Thomas Paine

With independence won, Paine left America for France, honoured and beloved. Congress had voted him money as had the State of Pennsylvania, and New York State gave him a farm in New Rochelle. He arrived in Paris in 1787, again with letters of introduction from Franklin, but he was already famous in France as the author of *Common Sense*.

From there he returned to England, and in London, at Clio Rickman's house, wrote *Rights of Man*, a book that so antagonised the government that he was forced to flee the country. He was charged with sedition for his attack on the Crown and escaped to a rapturous welcome in France, where he was welcomed with a triumphal procession.

He was granted French citizenship and elected to the National Convention, where he proceeded to draft a new constitution along the lines of the American republic.

COMMON SENSE:
ADDRESSED TO THE
INHABITANTS
OF
A M E R I C A.
On the following interesting
S U B J E C T S.

I. Of the Origin and Design of Government in general, with concise Remarks on the English Constitution.

II. Of Monarchy and Hereditary Succession.

III. Thoughts on the present State of American Affairs.

IV. Of the present Ability of America, with some miscellaneous Reflections.

Written by an ENGLISHMAN.
By Thomas Paine

Man knows no Master save creating HEAVEN;
Or those whom choice and common good ordain.
THOMSON.

PHILADELPHIA, Printed.
And Sold by R. BELL, in Third-Street, 1776.

Title page of Common Sense

28

Across the Channel in his homeland, anyone selling or possessing his book was liable to a fine, imprisonment or transportation. Particular offence was caused by the following passage, which refers to the line of German-speaking monarchs that had governed the country for almost all of the century:

> 'The time is not very far distant when England will laugh at itself for sending to Holland, Hanover, Zell, or Brunswick for men, at the expense of a million a year, who understand neither her laws, her language, nor her interest, and whose capacities would scarcely have fitted them for the office of parish constable.'

In France republicanism turned to violence and the bloodbath of the Reign of Terror began. Every day Paine witnessed friends marched to the guillotine. He was one of a small group who tried unsuccesfully to save Louis XVI, on the grounds that the monarch had helped America with money and alms. The king, he said, should be exiled to the United States, where he had friends, not sent to the guillotine.

Paine's ideas of rights, justice and mercy, were scorned by Robespierre and he was thrown into the Luxembourg Prison, where he languished for eleven months. While incarcerated he drafted the book that would alienate his remaining friends in England, and all of America – *The Age of Reason*. This poured scorn on the church establishment, organised religion and the doctrines of the Bible. Paine applied logic to the Bible as he had to politics. He was vilified as an atheist, when in fact he had become a deist. In France he had founded the Church of Theophilanthropy, whose members believed in the existence of God and the immortality of the soul, but not the divinity of Christ.

In England a proclamation was made against 'seditious writings', which included, of course, *Rights of Man*. In Sussex, where Paine was considered a front-runner in the carnage in France, effigies of him were hung from gibbets and consigned to bonfires. Dr John Delap, 1725-1812, of South Street, Lewes,

When the Almighty shall have blest us and made us a people dependent wholly upon Him, then may our first gratitude be shown by an act of continental legislation, which shall put a stop to the importation of Negroes for sale, soften the hard fate of those already here, and in time procure their freedom.

Thomas Paine

The obverse and reverse of a token used by an eighteenth century card player. On the side with the gibbet the inscription reads: END OF PAIN and on the other: MAY THE KNAVE OF JACOBIN CLUBS NEVER GET A TRICK.

vicar for nearly fifty years of Kingston-with-Iford, denounced Paine in an ode called *Sedition*.

Anti-republican feeling ran high in the county town, although there remained pockets of the radicalism that had marked Lewes for a century or more. One 'riotous' radical of the time was Paul Dunvan, the anonymous author of *Ancient and Modern History of Lewes and Brighthelmston* (1795); another, James Drowley, a Baptist lay preacher, emigrated to America in 1794, bought land at Sing Sing in New York State, and founded the town of Sparta.

Americans living in Paris petitoned unsuccessfully for Paine's release in January 1794. He had yearned for America while imprisoned, and was hurt that the government of the country for which he had fought with pen and sword had made no effort to rescue him.

A report in the (English) *Morning Advertiser* for February 8, 1794, says:

'In the sittings of the French Convention of the 7th of January, a deputation of Americans were admitted to the bar, and the orator requested the pardon of Thomas Paine, the Apostle of Liberty, who had been proscribed in England, whose arrest was a species of triumph to all the tyrants on earth. . . .They requested, therefore, with confidence, that Thomas Paine should be restored to the fraternal embrace of his fellow citizens, and they offered themselves sureties for his conduct during the short time that he should remain in France.'

The convention promised to consider the request, and eventually Paine was released. He remained in France for a few years more as it was unsafe to return to England, where he would have faced arrest for sedition. Robespierre was executed and the Terror came to an end in 1794. Paine witnessed the rise of Napoleon Buonaparte and the end of his hopes for an egalitarian society.

Nineteen years after he left America he decided to return to what he considered his real home. He landed on October 30,

1802, at Baltimore, his money gone, his health broken by imprisonment – and he was ignored. Said David McLean: 'The *Age of Reason* had stirred the depths of such a nest of hornets as would buzz and sting him until he died. He had attacked with scorn dogmas held sacred; he had dared to declare that, if the Bible were to be believed, God was a monster, who butchered men and women and children, without pity or remorse. He was denounced as "an emissary from Satan".'

Every religious denomination was against him, from the Quakers to the Roman Catholics. For decades to come he was maligned by clergymen who preached against Paine's 'vulgar atheism', and as late as the twentieth century Theodore Roosevelt called him 'a filthy little atheist'.

At Trenton, which his first *Crisis* pamphlet had saved, he was refused a seat in the stage-coach; he was hooted and insulted. The hardest blow of all was when, at New Rochelle, where Paine owned a farm, he was refused a vote in the elections, on the grounds that *he was not an American citizen*.

I believe in one God and no more, and I hope for happiness beyond this life.
Thomas Paine

He died on June 8 1809, aged seventy-two, at a house in Columbia Street, Greenwich Village in New York. His body was ulcerated, his feet blistered and he had suffered from dropsy. His request to be interred at the Quaker burial ground was refused by the Society of Friends, and his body was carried twenty-five miles for burial at his farm in New Rochelle.

His will closed with these words: 'I die in perfect composure, and resignation to the will of my Creator, God.'

RIGHTS OF MAN:

BEING AN

ANSWER TO MR. BURKE's ATTACK

ON THE

FRENCH REVOLUTION.

BY

THOMAS PAINE,

SECRETARY FOR FOREIGN AFFAIRS TO CONGRESS IN THE
AMERICAN WAR, AND
AUTHOR OF THE WORK INTITLED *COMMON SENSE,*

LONDON:
PRINTED FOR J. JOHNSON, St. PAUL's CHURCH-YARD.
MDCCXCI.

Title page of Rights of Man

31

CALUMNY AND

VILIFICATION

Peace, which costs nothing, is attended with infinitely more advantage than any victory with all its expenses.
Thomas Paine

In the final seven years of his life – old, tired, ill, rejected and ignored – Paine drank too much. During this time he was the victim of virulent and successful political propaganda by his two earliest, and most hostile, biographers, Francis Oldys (the pen name of George Chalmers) whose book came out in 1791, the year of publication of *Rights of Man*, and James Cheetham, who published in 1809, the year of Paine's death. For a century or more afterwards their vitriolic attacks were the basis of the legend that Paine was a drunken profligate, debauched and intemperate. He was vilifed and abused, the object of calumny, and ridiculed as 'Tom Paine the stay-maker'.

His friend, Joel Barlow, had told a prospective biographer shortly after Paine's death that then was not the time to publish such a book.

'The greatest part of the readers in the United States will not be persuaded as long as their present feelings last, to consider him in any other light than as a drunkard and a deist. The writer of his life who should dwell on these topics, to the exclusion of the great and estimable traits of his real character, might, indeed, please the rabble of the age who do not know him. The book might sell; but it would only tend to render the truth more obscure for the future biographer than it was before.'

Barlow's advice was prophetic, for that is indeed what Paine's first biographers did. As late as 1870, the eminent Sussex historian Mark Antony Lower, in his *Compendious History of Sussex*, called Paine 'the atheistical writer of the "Age of Reason"'. Said Lower: 'He wrote that execrable book in this house (Bull House), and the table on which he wrote it was, about fifty years since, in the possession of the late William Lee of this town'. In fact, *Age of Reason* was begun while Paine was in prison in France, and the first part was published in 1794, twenty years after Paine left Lewes.

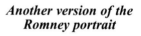

Yet, despite the remorseless attacks made upon Paine over the years since his death, his writings have continued to lead succeeding generations to aspire to his ideals. Some feel there is still a lack of an adequate biography. 'A fair assessment of Paine will necessitate the combined efforts of several contributors, each an expert in one of the fields in which Paine achieved prominence,' the Thomas Paine Society believes.

My own mind is my Church.
Thomas Paine

Another version of the Romney portrait

In 1819 William Cobbett (who, as Peter Porcupine – an emigrant to America – had ridiculed Paine while he lived, and who later became a disciple) arranged for Paine's bones to be disinterred and returned to England. He planned for the remains to form the heart of a great monument to Paine.

A Dr Francis, quoted by Conway, wrote:

'A singular coincidence led me to pay a visit to Cobbett at his country seat, within a couple of miles of the city, on the island, on the very day that he had exhumed the bones of Paine, and shipped them for England. I will here repeat the words which Cobbett gave utterance to at the friendly interview our party

33

'The Policital CHAMPION turned Resurrection Man!'
William Cobbett returns to England with Paine's bones.
© THE BRITISH MUSEUM

had with him. "I have just performed a duty, gentlemen, which has been too long delayed: you have neglected too long the remains of Thomas Paine. I have done myself the honour to disinter his bones. I have removed them from New Rochelle. I have dug them up; they are now on their way to England. When I myself return, I shall cause them to speak the common sense of the great man; I shall gather together the people of Liverpool and Manchester in one assembly with those of London, and those bones will effect the reformation of England in Church and State.'"

Paine's bones were landed at Liverpool on November 21, 1819, but Cobbett's proposed monument never materialised. After Cobbett died the bones passed in 1836 into the hands of a receiver. The Lord Chancellor refused to regard them as an

34

asset. Hypatia Bradlaugh Bonner, who edited Conway's posthumous 1909 book about Paine, wrote that the bones were kept by 'an old day-labourer' until 1844, when they passed to furniture dealer B Tilley of Bedford Square, London. In 1849 the empty coffin was in the possession of J Chennell of Guildford. The silver plate bore the inscription 'Thomas Paine, died June 8, 1809, aged 72'. In 1854 the Reverend R Anslie claimed to own 'the skull and right hand of Thomas Paine'.

Today, there is no trace of Paine's bones. A legend says that one of his little fingers was left in American soil. Beneath a monument to Paine in New Rochelle is said to be a box containing a fragment of Paine's brain and hair 'which after wandering about the world ever since Cobbett brought Paine's remains to England, was purchased in 1900 by Dr. Moncure Conway, and which through his devotion has, we may hope, found at last a final resting place,' according to Hypatia Bradlaugh Bonner.

In July 1999 the *Sussex Express* carried a report that Paine's skull had been found in Australia, but the claim has yet to be substantiated.

Monarchy . . . is the popery of Government; a thing well kept up to amuse the ignorant, and quiet them into taxes.

Thomas Paine

Tom Paine's skull found in Australia

Says the man from the Western Front

Sussex Express, July 2, 1999

THOMAS PAINE TERRITORY

(See page 48 for map)

BULL HOUSE

In ancient times, says a tablet on the east wall of Bull House, 'the Bull Inn with the Westgate Chapel was held of the barony of Lewes at the yearly rent of a race of ginger'. The building dates from *c*1450.

The inn was bought by Sir Henry Goring in 1583 from Thomas Matthews, a Lewes yeoman, for £160. Sir Henry enlarged the property and transformed it into a town house for himself and his family. He died in 1595, leaving it to his son Edward, who sold it in 1612 to Edward Claggett of Portslade. Three years later Claggett sold the Bull for £325 to Thomas Oliver, a Lewes merchant. It remained in the possession of the Oliver family until 1698 when it was bought by Thomas Adams of Meeching for £210 and sold again in the same year, for the same price, to the Reverend Thomas Barnard.

Barnard gutted the southern block, added by Sir Henry Goring, leaving only the outer shell, to form Westgate Chapel. He sold the remainder, which included the original Bull Inn, to John Ollive, his succeeding minister of Westgate Chapel. After Ollive's death the house passed into the ownership of his son Samuel.

Bull House is now owned by the Sussex Archaeological Society, which has offices on the ground floor and part of the first floor. The rest is privately occupied. The house is considerably larger than it appears from the High Street, is very heavily timbered internally and contains a number of surprisingly light and spacious rooms, some with unexpected views of town and Downs.

The first floor front room, believed to be Paine's parlour, has, as well as a large window looking over the High Street, two small east and west windows that give views down the High Street and to Cliffe Hill beyond, and up through 'the bottleneck'– the twist in the road at Westgate. A back room on the ground floor has a massive inglenook fireplace, and set in its hearth is a tobacco mill wheel found on the premises and believed to be one used by Paine. Two quaint satyrs in carved oak, from Goring's time, support the beams of the first floor.

An outhouse Paine put up on the west side of Bull House, possibly for the storage of groceries or for housing a mill, caused a problem for his neighbours at Westgate Chapel in 1772, and on July 18 he wrote a letter of apology.

Bull House The main door and the satyrs supporting the first floor

FROM A DRAWING BY RUTH COBB IN TRAVELLERS TO THE TOWN, 1953

'I do hereby confess myself under an Obligation of paying the sum of One shilling yearly to the Trustees

37

Westgate Chapel, with Bull House on the left

of the dissenters Meeting House situated in the Parish of St. Michael Lewes in an acknowledgement for their suffering the droppings of Rain which fall from a New Building lately erected by me, to fall into a Yard belonging and adjoining to the North side of the said Meeting House.'

Bull House was restored by Alderman John Every in 1922.

WESTGATE CHAPEL

Many of Paine's biographers have described Samuel Ollive as a Quaker. In fact he was a nonconformist, who worshipped at Westgate Chapel where his father John had been a minister. He also attended services at St-Michael-in-Lewes.

Following the Act of Uniformity, 1662, dissenting clergymen from the churches of St Anne and St Michael were removed from their livings. With some of their congregations they formed nonconformist groups, one of which settled at Westgate Chapel. The Reverend Thomas Barnard had the chapel on November 5, 1700. John Ollive was minister from 1711 to 1740.

Thomas Paine and Elizabeth Ollive were married across the road at St Michael's because at that time nonconformist ministers were not permitted to conduct marriage ceremonies.

Thomas Walker Horsfield, the Sussex antiquarian, was minister at Westgate from 1817 to 1827.

In 1913 the meeting-house was sub-divided and arranged as a chapel, a hall and a vestibule. A Fair Trade shop is today held in the hall for two hours on Thursday, Friday and Saturday and for an hour on Sunday.

WHITE HART HOTEL

The White Hart likes to regard itself as 'the cradle of American independence'. It is a sixteenth century building, originally the town house of the Pelham family, and it became an inn two hundred years later when the Pelhams were elevated to the peerage. As the Dukes of Newcastle they moved across the the road to Newcastle House.

The balconied Sheriff's Room is where the Headstrong Club met in Paine's day. It is still panelled with the original sixteenth century timbers and has been used at times in the recent past by a reconvened Headstrong Club.

The hotel in the nineteenth century

39

The bowling green in the castle tilting yard

FROM A DRAWING BY JAT 1963

LEWES BOWLING GREEN

The venerable bowling green within the castle precincts vies with the White Hart Hotel as the hypothetical site where the seeds of revolution in America were sown in Paine's mind.

Thomas Paine was a talented player who 'observed much more exactness with the measuring-stick, than he was accustomed to do at the beer-barrel with his dipping-rule'.

Lewes Bowling Green Society was founded in 1753 by Charles Boore, keeper of The Castle inn, 'for the better management of the old Castle Green on which the game of bowls has been played since time immemorial'.

The ground had been, centuries earlier, the castle's tilting (jousting) yard. The version of bowls played here in Paine's time, and still played today, is that by which Drake whiled away the hours at Plymouth Ho in 1588 as he awaited the

Spanish Armada. Lewes bowls, an eccentric game played only by men, has nothing in common with the modern game played on municipal greens by elderly people in white polyester.

No velvet greensward, the pitch is a daisy-starred, odd and irregular piece of grass with a definite slope from one side to the other. During the Second World War part of it was excavated for an air raid shelter, and another part for a static water tank. With post-war restoration, it acquired an interesting new collection of lumps and bumps. To compensate for the peculiarities of the green, players use bowls of a considerably heavier bias than those played on modern greens. It is said that some of the bowls, if cast wide on favourable ground, are quite capable of approaching the jack from behind. In the Lewes game, the jacks are the same shape and material as the bowls, and have a similar bias.

The society owns a number of battle-scarred woods dating from before Paine's time, with which he would have played.

ST MICHAEL-IN-LEWES

Here Thomas Paine was married to Elizabeth Ollive on March 26, 1771. The witnesses were Elizabeth's brother, Thomas, and Paine's friend, Henry Verrall. The curate, Robert Austen, mis-spelled the Ollives' name on the marriage certificate, by giving it only one 'l', and he also described Paine (then still known as Pain) as a 'Bachelor'. Did Elizabeth, or the curate, know of his first marriage?

Paine's father-in-law, Samuel Ollive, the nonconformist, was also a seat-holder at St Michael's. He occupied pew number twenty-seven. Those elected to public office, as Ollive was, were required to be members of the Church of England.

The tower and the west wall of the church are all that remain of the original thirteenth century building. The unusual round tower is one of only three (the others are at Southease and Piddinghoe, south of Lewes), and this one has been

St Michael-in-Lewes from the back

somewhat vandalised by a thick coating of pebble-dash. The tower is topped by a twisted, shingled spire, and carries a sculpture of St Michael. This is the work of Harry Phillips, and dates from 1976.

The church was rebuilt in the fourteenth century and again in 1748 when the south wall of squared, knapped flints, with two entrance doors, was built. This was the facade Paine would have known, and seen daily from his parlour window. Squaring and knapping flints was, even then, a tremendously costly business, and was undertaken in this instance to demonstrate the church's wealth.

A century later the inelegant Church House, which carries the Town Clock, was added.

Behind St Michael's is a 'secret' churchyard, unseen and unsuspected by passers-by, where dappled sunshine filtering through ancient trees falls on extravagantly rampant old roses, and where there is quite the best view in town of the castle – seen across its dry moat.

Squared, knapped flints on the south wall of the church

MARKET TOWER

This handsome brick tower was built in 1792 for use as a provision market. In its belfry hangs Gabriel, the sixteenth century town bell, which is rung on portentous occasions. Market Tower is shabby and neglected. Its upper rooms are used as a store and rehearsal room by an amateur operatic society and the old market space is now merely a short cut between the High Street and Market Lane. It is dank, cold, dirty and, during the day, the furtive haven of outcast shop and office workers who need a smoke.

In a brick niche is a superb painting of Paine by Julian Bell. Paine is shown with upraised arm pointing west to America. Behind him is Lewes, and over his right shoulder the River Seine snakes towards Paris, where the Bastille is burning.

Market Tower

Ignominiously carted off – the unpopular collage

SUSSEX EXPRESS

The painting, affectionately regarded by Lewesians (and, regrettably, the regular target of moustache-painters), replaces an earlier work, in the form of a collage, commissioned by the new Headstrong Club and presented to the town in 1993. This attracted much ribald comment and was removed from the Market Tower fourteen months later and placed in the All Saints Centre, Friars Walk, Lewes.

Julian Bell's offer of a painting for the niche was gratefully accepted by the tower's owner, Lewes Town Council.

Julian Bell puts the finishing touches to his painting ANGUS HOY

43

HARVEYS BREWERY

Harveys Brewery in the Cliffe

Harveys makes a splendid Tom Paine strong pale ale, brewed to the old traditional standards. It was first made in July 1993 – to honour Thomas Paine; to mark July 4, Independence Day in the USA; and also to celebrate the Campaign for Real Ale's first Independent Brewers' Month.

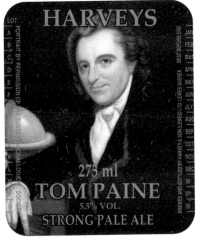

Tom Paine Strong Pale Ale is exported to the United States where customers particularly appreciate the advertising poster, on which the message is: 'A taste of independence'.

The ale is available in bottle form all year round from the brewery shop in the Cliffe. In July it is available draught in Harvey pubs.

Label for Harveys'
Tom Paine pale ale

OTHER PLACES OF INTEREST IN LEWES

LEWES CASTLE Begun immediately after the Norman Conquest of 1066, Lewes Castle is one of the oldest in England. It was built by William de Warenne as part of a chain of fortifications to defend vital routes between England and Normandy. After the last de Warenne died in 1347 the castle was abandoned and fell into decay. It was broken into by a mob during the Peasants' Revolt in 1381 and badly damaged; thereafter townspeople carted off its materials for their own buildings. Gradually, over the centuries, parts of the castle and its grounds were built upon so that eventually all that remained were the Norman gatehouse, the fourteenth century Barbican and the ruined shell keep. The castle is open to visitors daily.

PRIORY OF ST PANCRAS The priory, mother house of the Cluniac order in England, was built by the pious William de Warenne and his wife Gundrada. Work began in 1077. In 1264 Henry III lodged at the priory before and after the seminal Battle of Lewes in 1264

Above, mermorial to the Battle of Lewes in the grounds of Lewes Priory

(which led to the foundation of parliamentary government). At the Dissolution it was the wealthiest Cluniac house in England. The extensive buildings covered thirty acres and the priory owned 20,000 acres in Sussex, estates in other counties, seven daughter houses and 19 parish churches. Henry VIII, he of the six wives, broke with the Pope, renounced the Catholic church and ordered closure of the monasteries.

Ruins of the Priory of St Pancras

In 1538 the King's minister, Thomas Cromwell, hired Italian engineer John Portinari to demolish the great buildings.

Little remains. Impressively massive ruins delineate the infirmary chapel, the rere-dorter, the dorter and refectory. Stone from the priory ruins may be seen in many Lewes buildings. When excavations were made across the site for the railway line in 1845, the graves of William and Gundrada were uncovered. Lead cists containing their remains may be seen in Southover Church.

AMONG BOOKS AND PAPERS CONSULTED:

Colin Brent, *Georgian Lewes*, Colin Brent Books, 1993
JM Connell, *Thomas Paine*, Longmans, Green and Co, 1939
Moncure Daniel Conway, *The Life of Thomas Paine*, edited
    Hypatia Bradlaugh Bonner, Watts 1909
Samuel Edwards, *Rebel!*, New English Library, 1974
David Freeman Hawke, *Paine*, WW Norton (US) 1974
Jack Fruchtman Jr, *Thomas Paine*, Four Walls Eight
    Windows (US) 1994
Audrey Williamson, *Thomas Paine*, George Allen and
    Unwin, 1973
The Life of Paine, 'Editor of The National', Watson, 1842
The Game of Bowls at the Tilting Ground, Lewes (booklet), 1968
Sussex County Magazine, 1930
Leaflets, pamphlets, papers in the Sussex Room of Lewes
    Library and in Sussex Archaeological Society's library

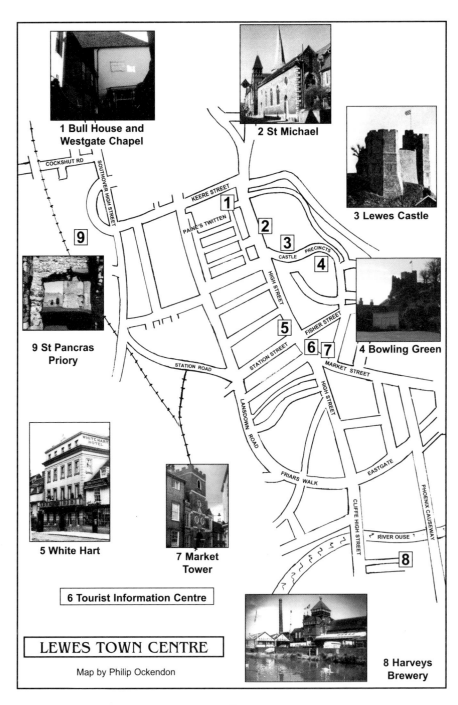

1 Bull House and Westgate Chapel

2 St Michael

3 Lewes Castle

9 St Pancras Priory

4 Bowling Green

5 White Hart

7 Market Tower

6 Tourist Information Centre

LEWES TOWN CENTRE

Map by Philip Ockendon

8 Harveys Brewery

48